Pearson Edexcel GCE English Literature

Component 1a: Drama
Shakespeare Critical Anthology: Tragedy

For use with:

A level English Literature (9ET0) Component 1a – Drama (Shakespeare)

Published by Pearson Education Limited, a company incorporated in England and Wales, having its registered office at Edinburgh Gate, Harlow, Essex, CM20 2JE. Registered company number: 872828

Edexcel is a registered trade mark of Edexcel Limited

© Pearson Education Limited 2014

First published 2014

17 16 15
10 9 8 7 6 5 4

British Library Cataloguing in Publication Data
A catalogue record for this book is available from the British Library

ISBN 9781446913499

Printed in the UK by ESP Colour Ltd

Cover images: *Background*: **123RF.com**: Theepatheep Kawinpathawee; *Masks*: **Shutterstock.com:** InnervisionArt

Acknowledgements

We are grateful to the following for permission to reproduce copyright material:

Section A: Tragedy

1 David Scott Kastan, '"A rarity most beloved": Shakespeare and the Idea of Tragedy', in *A Companion to Shakespeare's Works Vol I*, Blackwell 2003
2 A. D. Nuttall, 'Aristotle and After', in *Why Does Tragedy Give Pleasure?*, OUP 1996
3 A. C. Bradley, 'The Substance of Shakespearean Tragedy', in *Shakespearean Tragedy*, Penguin 1991
4 Maynard Mack, 'What Happens in Shakespearean Tragedy', in *Everybody's Shakespeare: Reflections Chiefly on the Tragedies*, University of Nebraska Press 1993

Section B: *Antony and Cleopatra*

1 Howard Jacobson, '*Antony and Cleopatra*: Gentle Madam, No', in *Shakespeare's Magnanimity*, OUP 1987
2 Emrys Jones, 'Introduction', in *Antony and Cleopatra*, Penguin 1977
3 Tony Tanner, in *Prefaces to Shakespeare*, Harvard University Press 1993

Section C: *Hamlet*

1 John Kerrigan, in *Revenge Tragedy: Aeschylus to Armageddon*, Clarendon 1996
2 Janet Adelman, 'Man and Wife Is One Flesh: *Hamlet* and the Confrontation with the Maternal Body', in *Suffocating Mothers*, Routledge 1992
3 William Hazlitt, '*Hamlet*' in *Characters of Shakespeare's Plays*, OUP 1916

Section D: *King Lear*

1 Carol Rutter, 'Eel Pie and Ugly Sisters in *King Lear*', in *Lear from Study to Stage*, Associated University Presses 1997
2 Frank Kermode, '*King Lear*', in *Shakespeare's Language*, Allen Lane 2000
3 Fintan O'Toole, '*King Lear*: Zero Hour' in *Shakespeare Is Hard, But So Is Life*, Granta 2002

Section E: *Othello*

1 E. A. J. Honigmann, 'Introduction', in *Othello*, Arden 3rd Series 2001
2 F. R. Leavis, 'Diabolical Intellect and the Noble Hero', in Scrutiny, December 1937
3 Ania Loomba, '*Othello* and the Radical Question', in *Shakespeare, Race, and Colonialism*, OUP 1998

Every effort has been made to contact copyright holders to obtain their permission for the use of copyright material. Pearson Education will, if notified, be happy to rectify any errors or omissions and include any such rectifications in future editions.

Contents

Introduction   4

Section A: Tragedy

   1 Shakespearean tragedy   6

   2 The pleasure of tragedy   8

   3 The Shakespearean tragic hero   10

   4 Tragedy and madness   12

Section B: *Antony and Cleopatra*

   1 Antony's suicide   14

   2 *Antony and Cleopatra*: the play's structure   16

   3 Time and timelessness in *Antony and Cleopatra*   18

Section C: *Hamlet*

   1 Memory and remembrance in *Hamlet*   20

   2 Hamlet: Avenging his father or saving his mother?   22

   3 The complexity of Hamlet   24

Section D: *King Lear*

   1 Language and female power in *King Lear*   26

   2 Ways of speaking in *King Lear*   28

   3 The morality of *King Lear*   31

Section E: *Othello*

   1 *Othello*: The portrayal of Iago   33

   2 The character of Othello   35

   3 *Othello*, race and society   37

The Edexcel Shakespeare Critical Anthology

Introduction

At the heart of Edexcel's A level Literature specification is the literary text. Teachers and academics tell us that, above all, A level should encourage you to read and re-read your literary texts and to know them well. They also want students to read widely, deeply and independently to secure informed views about these texts. Reading critically means not just having opinions, but seeing that other readers might think differently.

This collection of critical passages is designed to extend and illuminate your reading of your set Shakespeare play. It results from our extensive research to understand what teachers and university English departments really believe are the most important skills and knowledge for students of literature at A level. The critical views contained here will offer you a range of perspectives on tragedy, as well as three specific passages on your chosen Shakespeare play. In total you will have seven passages that are relevant to your A level Shakespeare text (Component 1 – Drama).

The texts have been selected to give you a taste of high-quality writing by literary critics about a text that you should know well. They have been chosen by academics at one of the leading university English departments in the country, University College London, led by Professor John Mullan. Teachers may wish to supplement them with other passages of criticism that they think are illuminating, but this is not essential. We hope that your own critical writing style will be enriched by reading, and sometimes grappling with, these tightly crafted pieces by skilled literary thinkers. The arguments posed will enable you to consider the views of others and form, and perhaps re-assess, your own readings of your studied Shakespeare play.

So how might you use literary criticism within A level Literature? This will vary from student to student, depending on your developing skills in the subject. There is no expectation for you to pepper your own responses to Shakespeare with quotations from this anthology, or to ensure that a set percentage of your essay references this material. The intention is that your own responses to Shakespeare's writing will be enriched by considering the range of viewpoints offered here. Think of reading this criticism as rather like having a conversation; we offer each of these perspectives not as 'the answer' to reading Shakespeare, but merely as another reading of the text for you to engage with. You may find that some of the critics do not seem to agree with each other.

All of the points below are valuable ways of using the extended reading offered in this collection – during class discussion, in personal essays, or ultimately in your examination responses:

- Understand the interpretation being put forward about the literary text(s).
- Compare the critic's position with your own reading of the text (or indeed that of another critic or a member of your class). Identify any points of connection or difference.
- Agree with the point made. Identify further evidence in Shakespeare's text to extend it.
- Disagree with the critic's position. Identify evidence in Shakespeare's text that might support your opposing argument.
- Refine the critic's position. Identify one element that you can support and another that you would prefer to refine and qualify with evidence from the text.
- Select particular quotations that support or contrast with your own reading of the text to strengthen your discussion or literary essay.

Remember that, for all today's students, with ready access to the internet, the issue of plagiarism is an important one. You can, and should, draw on both the literary text and your wider reading to craft your own arguments. However, once you use others' words, or specific ideas, you must acknowledge them by use of a footnote or bracketed reference within your text. While Shakespeare borrowed many of his stories from other writers, academic essay-writing must be your own!

UCL
Professor John Mullan, Professor Helen Hackett and Professor René Weis

Pearson
Katy Lewis, Esther Menon

Section A: Tragedy
1 Shakespearean tragedy

Kastan sees Shakespeare's tragedies as intense treatments of age-old questions about whether the causes of suffering lie in human weakness, divine retribution, or arbitrary fate. He asserts that the absence of clear answers to these questions is central to Shakespearean tragedy. While Shakespeare did not have a fully worked-out theory of tragedy, his coherent and powerful sense of tragedy develops and deepens with each tragic play.

If any theoretical pressures existed to shape Shakespeare's understanding of tragedy they came more from medieval articulations of the genre than classical ones. Chaucer was seemingly the first to use the English word "tragedy," in a gloss in his translation (ca. 1380) of **Boethius's *De Consolatione Philosophiae***: "**Tragedye is to seyn a dite of a prosperite for a tyme that endeth in wrecchidnesse.**" The felt need for a gloss suggests that tragedy was then an unfamiliar concept in English, but quickly the idea of tragedy as the fall from prosperity to wretchedness became commonplace. Chaucer's definition is perhaps so limited as to seem obvious and unhelpful, especially in our **hypertheoretical** age, but in its very simplicity it calls attention to tragedy's power, marking it as universal and inexplicable. It defines the inescapable trajectory of the tragic action but not its cause, and in its reticence about who or what is responsible for the dire change of fortune it speaks tragedy's fearful incomprehensibility.

… Chaucer's definitional reserve finds its most powerful **analogue** in the agonizing silences of Shakespeare's tragedies. "Why should a dog, a horse, a rat have life / And thou no breath at all?" (5.8.307–8), King Lear cries, holding his broken child. No answer is forthcoming, though it lies in the incalculable murderousness of the world. And directly questioning that world produces no more satisfying responses. "Is there any cause in nature that makes these hard hearts?" (3.6.74–5).

Glossary

Boethius's *De Consolatione Philosophiae*   Boethius (480–524AD) was a Roman philosopher. The *Consolation of Philosophy*, written when Boethius was in prison, is an imaginary conversation between Boethius and Philosophy, who is depicted as a woman.

'Tragedye is to seyn a dite of a prosperite for a tyme that endeth in wrecchidnesse.'
'Tragedy means a literary composition written in happier times recalling events that ended in misery.'

hypertheoretical   tending to produce lots of theories

These are the unanswered (perhaps unanswerable) questions of the tragic world. Are there reasons for the intolerable suffering? Is the tragic motor human error or **capricious** fate? Is the catastrophe a just, if appalling, retribution, or an **arbitrary** destiny reflecting the indifference, or, worse, the **malignity** of the heavens? …

For Shakespeare, anyhow, the uncertainty is the point. Characters may commit themselves to a confident sense of the tragic world they inhabit; but the plays inevitably **render** that preliminary understanding inadequate, and the characters struggle unsuccessfully to reconstruct a coherent worldview from the ruins of the old. And it is the emotional truth of the struggle rather than the **metaphysical** truth of the worldview that is at the center of these plays. Shakespeare's tragedies provoke the questions about the cause of the pain and loss the plays so agonizingly portray, and in the refusal of any answers starkly prevent any confident attribution of meaning or value to human suffering.

Perhaps here we can begin to discover the logic of Shakespeare's tragic practice. Kenneth Muir's oft-quoted comment that "There is no such thing as Shakespearian tragedy: there are only Shakespearian tragedies" merely begs the question of how "Shakespearian" modifies "tragedy," either as an individual exemplar or a group. If Muir is only saying that Shakespeare does not seem to have written tragedy driven by a fully developed theoretical conception of the genre we can easily **assent**, but a coherent and powerfully compelling sense of tragedy can be seen to develop through the plays.

Tragedy, for Shakespeare, is the genre of **uncompensated** suffering, and as he writes in that mode the successive plays reveal an ever more profound formal acknowledgment of their **desolating** controlling logic.

From David Scott Kastan, '"A rarity most beloved": Shakespeare and the Idea of Tragedy', 2003.

analogue   parallel, or quality of being similar to something else

capricious   unpredictable

arbitrary   determined by chance or whim

malignity   quality of being highly dangerous; full of malice or hatred

render   to cause to become; make

metaphysical   theoretical or philosophical

assent   agree; consent

uncompensated   unrewarded; not compensated

desolating   devastating

2 The pleasure of tragedy

In this extract Nuttall considers the tension between pleasure and pain in tragic drama. Early critical responses to tragedy considered audience pleasure in relation to the pain they were witnessing on stage. Contemporary reviewers more commonly praise the playwright's ability to disturb the emotions of the audience and render them uncomfortable.

If we were all wicked, there would perhaps be no problem. A world of torturers would naturally be pleased by the blinding of **Oedipus** or else, to take a cooler form of wickedness, it would not be surprising if an audience inwardly driven by envy were to delight in the fall of one greater than they. But why does tragedy give pleasure to 'people like ourselves'?

A cruel or sadistic pleasure in the blinding of Oedipus is immediately distinguishable from what **Aristotle** called the *oikeia hedone*, 'the proper pleasure' of tragedy (*Poetics*, 1459 a 21) and I fancy that the same is true – though less obviously true – in the case of the gloating, envious spectator. In the tragic theatre suffering and death are perceived as matter for grief and fear, after which it seems that grief and fear become in their turn matter for enjoyment.

'The pleasure of tragedy' is an immediately uncomfortable phrase. Quite apart from the original basic collision between terrible matter and a delighted response, there is an awkwardness, somehow, in the very mildness of the term 'pleasure' – it seems a puny word to set beside the thunderous term 'tragedy' – adding a species of insult to injury. The **Nietzschean oxymoron**, 'tragic joy', is, oddly, easier to accept, because it fights fire with fire. I suspect moreover that the awkwardness has become more obvious in our century. For moral **Dr Johnson** it was self-evident that poetry and drama must please. A later kind of moralism taught a new generation of readers and theatre-goers to despise the pleasurable and to value the disturbing, the jagged, the painful work. It is now virtually unimaginable that a reviewer of a new play should praise it by saying that it offers solace or comfort. Conversely the adjective 'uncomfortable' is automatically read as

Glossary

Oedipus   According to Greek myth, after realising that he had fulfilled a prophecy that he would both kill his father and sleep with his mother, Oedipus blinded himself with two pins from his mother's dress.

Aristotle   Greek philosopher who in 335BC wrote *Poetics*, one of the first works of dramatic theory, in which he describes the features of drama and tragedy in particular

Nietzsche   German philosopher (1844–1900) who wrote *The Birth of Tragedy*, in which he argues that Greek tragedy helped early audiences appreciate their own existence

oxymoron   language device where two opposite words or meanings are used side by side, e.g. 'sour sweet'

Dr Johnson   Samuel Johnson (1709–84) was a poet, essayist, moralist and critic who compiled *A Dictionary of the English Language* (1755), which had a far-reaching effect on modern English.

praise. Ancient **Stoics** and **Epicureans** argued about most things but they would be united in their bewilderment at this. I am a twentieth-century person and I share the general taste for discomfort. But the radical problem remains obstinately in place: if people go again and again to see such things, they must in some way enjoy them. Similarly, if you like the disturbing kind of play then *this* disturbance is something you like, must itself be a further mode of pleasure. The shift in taste does not resolve the problem of tragic pleasure; rather it sets an allied, similarly challenging problem – that of enjoyed discomfort – alongside it.

Many things, when looked at hard, seem to come to bits (or, as we now say, 'to undergo deconstruction'). Certainly this is true of the notion of pleasure. 'Quantity of pleasure being equal, push-pin is as good as poetry,' said **Jeremy Bentham**, robustly. Here pleasure is offered for inspection as a luminously simple datum: of course poetry and push-pin are profoundly different things, but, meanwhile, pleasure is pleasure, *semper idem*. But the datum can prove strangely elusive. For example, while it may seem essential to the idea of pleasure that it be felt, pleasure need not occupy the foreground of *consciousness*, which will afford simultaneous space for objects of another kind. I mean by this only that one can enjoy an activity or process without at any point thinking consciously, 'I am enjoying this', or 'this is very agreeable'; instead one may be thinking only of the activity itself. When two people converse we may observe that they enjoyed the conversation intensely, but if *per impossibile* one obtained entry to their fields of consciousness one would never find at any point a separately introspected element, 'the pleasant', but instead an unbroken preoccupation with the subject of the conversation itself.

From A. D. Nuttall, 'Aristotle and After', 1996.

Stoics Stoicism was a belief system founded in Greece. Stoics believed that learning to control your own will and suppress your emotions was the only way to understand the meaning of the universe. They thought people were equal in the eyes of the gods.

Epicureans Followers of a system of beliefs based on the writings of the philosopher Epicurus, Epicureans believed that pleasure could only be gained by modest living and tranquillity. They thought the gods were neutral and did not wish to interfere in people's lives.

Jeremy Bentham British philosopher (1748–1832) who founded utilitarianism, a system of ethics based on 'the greatest happiness of the greatest number'

semper idem always the same

per impossibile through some impossible means

3 The Shakespearean tragic hero

More than a century after its first publication, A. C. Bradley's Shakespearean Tragedy continues to be respected and frequently quoted. In this extract, Bradley considers Shakespearean tragedy in relation to definitions of the genre offered by the ancient Greek writer Aristotle and by medieval writers. He argues that Shakespearean tragedy necessarily centres on a character of high rank and exceptional qualities who undergoes a reversal of fortune that leads to his own death and to a more general calamity.

In approaching our subject it will be best, without attempting to shorten the path by referring to famous theories of the drama, to start directly from the facts, and to collect from them gradually an idea of Shakespearean Tragedy. And first, to begin from the outside, such a tragedy brings before us a considerable number of persons (many more than the persons in a Greek play, unless the members of the Chorus are reckoned among them); but it is **pre-eminently** the story of one person, the 'hero', or at most of two, the 'hero' and 'heroine'. Moreover, it is only in the love-tragedies, *Romeo and Juliet* and *Antony and Cleopatra*, that the heroine is as much the centre of the action as the hero. The rest, including *Macbeth*, are single stars. So that, having noticed the peculiarity of those two dramas, we may henceforth, for the sake of **brevity**, ignore it, and may speak of the tragic story as being concerned primarily with one person.

The story, next, leads up to, and includes, the *death* of the hero. On the one hand (whatever may be true of tragedy elsewhere), no play at the end of which the hero remains alive is, in the full Shakespearean sense, a tragedy; and we no longer class *Troilus and Cressida* or *Cymbeline* as such, as did the editors of the Folio. On the other hand, the story depicts also the troubled part of the hero's life which precedes and leads up to his death; and an instantaneous death occurring by 'accident' in the midst of prosperity would not **suffice** for it. It is, in fact, essentially a tale of suffering and calamity conducting to death.

The suffering and calamity are, moreover, exceptional. They befall a conspicuous person. They are themselves of some striking kind. They are also, as a rule, unexpected, and contrasted with previous happiness or glory. A tale, for example, of a man slowly worn to death by disease, poverty, little cares, sordid vices, petty persecutions, however piteous or dreadful it might be, would not be tragic in the Shakespearean sense.

Such exceptional suffering and calamity, then, affecting the hero, and – we must now add – generally extending far and wide beyond him, so as to make the whole scene a scene of woe, are an essential ingredient in tragedy and a chief source of the tragic emotions, and especially of pity. But the proportions of this ingredient, and the direction taken by tragic pity, will naturally vary greatly. Pity, for example has a much larger part in *King Lear* than in *Macbeth*, and is directed in the one case chiefly to the hero, in the other chiefly to minor characters.

Glossary

pre-eminently mainly or to a very great degree

brevity shortness; use of few words

suffice be enough

Let us now pause for a moment on the ideas we have so far reached. They would more than suffice to describe the whole tragic fact as it presented itself to the medieval mind. To the medieval mind a tragedy meant a narrative rather than a play... A total reverse of fortune, coming unawares upon a man who 'stood in high degree', happy and apparently secure – such was the tragic fact to the medieval mind. It appealed strongly to common human sympathy and pity; it startled also another feeling, that of fear. It frightened men and awed them. It made them feel that man is blind and helpless, the plaything of an inscrutable power, called by the name of Fortune or some other name – a power which appears to smile on him for a little, and then on a sudden strikes him down in his pride.

Shakespeare's idea of the tragic fact is larger than this idea and goes beyond it; but it includes it, and it is worth while to observe the identity of the two in a certain point which is often ignored. Tragedy with Shakespeare is concerned always with persons of 'high degree'; often with kings or princes; if not, with leaders in the state like Coriolanus, Brutus, Antony; at the least, as in *Romeo and Juliet*, with members of great houses, whose quarrels are of public moment. There is a decided difference here between *Othello* and our three other tragedies, but it is not a difference of kind. Othello himself is no mere private person; he is the General of the Republic. At the beginning we see him in the Council Chamber of the Senate. The consciousness of his high position never leaves him. At the end, when he is determined to live no longer, he is as anxious as Hamlet not to be misjudged by the great world, and his last speech begins,

> *Soft you; a word or two before you go.*
> *I have done the state some service, and they know it.*

And this characteristic of Shakespeare's tragedies, though not the most vital, is neither external nor unimportant. The saying that every death-bed is the scene of the fifth act of a tragedy has its meaning, but it would not be true if the word 'tragedy' bore its dramatic sense. The pangs of despised love and the anguish of remorse, we say, are the same in a peasant and a prince; but, not to insist that they cannot be so when the prince is really a prince, the story of the prince, the triumvir, or the general, has a greatness and dignity of its own. His fate affects the welfare of a whole nation or empire; and when he falls suddenly from the height of earthly greatness to the dust, his fall produces a sense of contrast, of the powerlessness of man, and of the omnipotence – perhaps the caprice – of Fortune or Fate, which no tale of private life can possibly rival.

From A. C. Bradley, 'The Substance of Shakespearean Tragedy', 1991. (*First published as 'Lecture 1: The Substance of Shakespearean Tragedy', 1904*).

4 Tragedy and madness

Mack notes how frequently Shakespearean tragic heroes suffer madness or are associated with it. Madness often seems to be a form of divine punishment, but also brings with it special insight and freedom to speak the truth. This resembles Shakespeare's own use of art to reveal painful truths. Mack argues that art and madness both allow freedom of speech, but that their insights may be dismissed as merely fiction or nonsense.

I have kept to the end, and out of proper order, the most interesting of all the symbolic elements in the hero's second phase. This is his experience of madness. One discovers with some surprise, I think, how many of Shakespeare's heroes are associated with this disease…

What (if anything), one wonders, may this mean? Doubtless a sort of explanation can be found in Elizabethan psychological lore, which held that the excess of any passion approached madness, and in the general prevalence through **Seneca** and other sources, of the **adage**: *Quos vult perdere Jupiter dementat prius*. Furthermore, madness, when actually exhibited, was dramatically useful, as **Kyd** had shown. It was arresting in itself, and it allowed the combination in a single figure of tragic hero and buffoon, to whom could be accorded the licence of the allowed fool in speech and action.

Just possibly, however, there was yet more to it than this, if we may judge by Shakespeare's sketches of madness in *Hamlet* and *King Lear*. In both these, madness is to some degree a punishment or doom, corresponding to the adage. Lear prays to the heavens that he may not suffer madness, and Hamlet asks Laertes, in his apology before the duel, to overlook his conduct, since 'you must needs have heard, how I am punish'd / With a sore distraction'. It is equally obvious, however, that in both instances the madness has a further dimension, as insight, and this is true also of Ophelia. Ophelia, mad, is able to make awards of flowers to the King and Queen which are appropriate to frailties of which she cannot be supposed to have conscious knowledge. For the same reason, I suspect we do not need **Dover Wilson**'s radical displacement of Hamlet's entry in

Glossary

Seneca   Roman dramatist, philosopher and statesman (4BC–65AD) whose dramas were very influential and are thought to have been the inspiration for the 'Revenge Tragedy', popular in both the Renaissance and the Restoration periods

adage   proverb or saying

Quos vult perdere Jupiter dementat prius   'Those whom Jupiter wishes to destroy, he first drives mad'

Kyd   Thomas Kyd (1558–94) wrote *The Spanish Tragedy*, which is regarded as one of the first Revenge Tragedies.

Dover Wilson   20th-century British scholar of Renaissance drama, whose text *What Happens in Hamlet* (1935) is one of the most influential studies of the play. However, Wilson often deviated wildly from his own textual principles if they did not support his preferred reading of a scene.

II. ii, so as to enable him to overhear Polonius. It is enough that Hamlet wears, even if it is for the moment self-assumed, the **guise** of the madman. As such, he can be presumed to have intuitive unformulated awarenesses that reach the surface in free (yet relevant) associations, like those of Polonius with a fishmonger, Ophelia with **carrion**. Lear likewise is allowed free yet relevant associations. His great speech in Dover fields on the lust of women derives from the designs of Goneril and Regan on Edmund, of which he consciously knows nothing. Moreover, both he and Hamlet can be privileged in madness to say things – Hamlet about the corruption of human nature, and Lear about the corruption of the Jacobean social system (and by extension about all social systems whatever), which Shakespeare could hardly have risked apart from this licence. Doubtless one of the anguishes of being a great artist is that you cannot tell people what they and you and your common institutions are really like – when viewed absolutely – without being dismissed as insane. To communicate at all, you must acknowledge the opposing voice; for there always is an opposing voice, and it is as deeply rooted in your own nature as in your audience's.

Just possibly, therefore, the meaning of tragic madness for Shakespeare approximated the meaning that the legendary figure of **Cassandra** (whom Shakespeare had in fact put briefly on his stage in the second act of *Troilus and Cressida*) has held for so many artists since his time. Cassandra's madness, like Lear's and Hamlet's – possibly, also, like the madness *verbally* assigned to other Shakespearean tragic heroes – contains both punishment and insight. She is doomed to know, by a consciousness that moves to measures outside our normal space and time; she is doomed never to be believed, because those to whom she speaks can hear only the opposing voice. With the language of the god Apollo sounding in her brain, and the incredulity of her fellow mortals ringing in her ears, she makes an ideal emblem of the predicament of the Shakespearean tragic hero, caught as he is between the **absolute** and the **expedient**. And by the same token, of the predicament of the artist – Shakespeare himself, perhaps – who, having been given the power to see the 'truth', can convey it only through poetry – what we commonly call a 'fiction', and dismiss.

From Maynard Mack, 'What Happens in Shakespearean Tragedy', 1993.

guise disguise; pretence

carrion dead or rotting flesh

Cassandra In Greek mythology, Cassandra had the power to see into the future (prophecy) but she was destined never to be believed.

absolute complete; perfect; all-powerful

expedient appropriate (especially in an urgent situation)

Section B: *Antony and Cleopatra*
1 Antony's suicide

This extract concerns the suicide of Antony after his forces have been defeated by Caesar at the Battle of Actium. It discusses why Shakespeare makes it so difficult for Antony to do this, arguing that the indignity of the scene is a consequence of the devotion that Antony has earlier required from his men.

Antony, as we have seen, has not been good at **steeling** men for a long time now; making them weep is where he is strong. Eros is already well softened when Antony puts his awful request to him, and his initial reluctance is countered thus:

> Eros,
> Wouldst thou be window'd in great Rome, and see
> Thy master thus with pleach'd arms, bending down
> His corrigible neck, his face subdued
> To penetrative shame; whilst the wheel'd seat
> Of fortunate Caesar, drawn before him, branded
> His baseness that ensued?

There is a strange, rather fleshly vividness in Antony's conjured image of himself and his shame here – 'pleach'd arms', 'corrigible neck', 'face subdued to penetrative shame'. It is an effect partly of imagining the compassion that there is to be felt on his behalf by another, of his knowing perhaps too well what a devotion to his own person is like and where it is susceptible. We might pass over in silence the success with which Antony reverses what we normally mean by sympathetic imaginativeness. But the speech is, for its further purpose, a failure; he makes himself, for anyone who loves him – and who indeed doesn't? – supremely unkillable…

Shakespeare might be plucking at our nerves when he has Antony botch his suicide, but there is nothing arbitrary about Antony's inability to find anyone who will mercifully – it's no longer a question of nobility – kill him. The excruciating indignities that attend his last hours are the price he pays for having made himself too much a man, too much a thing of emotion: for his followers an object of too piteous and reverential a love. Our moral sense easily accommodates the idea that penalties attach to hardness of heart; we are more reluctant to believe that nature also penalises its opposite. But could anything be more pointed than the preparedness of his guards to offer **laments** over a half-alive Antony, but not put an end to his pain?

Glossary

steeling creating a hard and resilient character or attitude

laments expressions of sorrow

First Guard	*What's the noise?*
Antony	*I have done my work ill, friends: O make an end*
	Of what I have begun.
Second Guard	*The star is fall'n.*
First Guard	*And time is at his period.*
All	*Alas, and woe!*
Antony	*Let him that loves me, strike me dead.*
First Guard	*Not I.*
Second Guard	*Nor I.*
Third Guard	*Nor any one.*
	(Exeunt Guards)

The tributes and the tears that have flowed so freely through the play flow still; but their crazy inappropriateness here, their being the last things Antony now requires, their positive hindrance of what he does want, is given us with the sharp apparentness of something close to farce. Here is devotion indeed! Everyone, it seems, is too beautifully devoted to Antony to help him. 'Let him that loves me, strike me dead' – he might have fared better with an appeal to loyalties less warm and affections less intimate. As it is he could not have fared worse. There is more than just the prudence of the ordinary soldier in the frantic refusal and dispersal of the guards; they shy from Antony as from some untouchable. The murderous instincts that a Macbeth or Coriolanus calls up might strike us as paying, after all, a greater tribute. They certainly pay a more serviceable one. He who lives by the sword shall die by the sword; he who lives by love enjoys the same justice but dies at the hands of a crueller **antagonist**.

From Howard Jacobson, '*Antony and Cleopatra:* Gentle Madam, No', 1987. *(First published as same in 1978).*

antagonist opponent; enemy

2 *Antony and Cleopatra*: the play's structure

> *Jones discusses the dramatic structure of the play. It boasts more scenes – many of them very short – than any other Shakespeare play. He attributes this to Shakespeare's desire to deliver a more detached, at times even ironic, perspective on the protagonists and the action. The play's scenic structure becomes a game of point and counterpoint; we are urged to measure reality against perception by a series of dramatic snapshots.*

Antony and Cleopatra heaves ripplingly like the sea in a quiet mood. Most of its scenes are short and **circumscribed**; they have no room for the grander movements of feeling, such as occur in most of the other great tragedies (like the forum scene in *Julius Caesar* or the temptation scene in *Othello*). With one possible exception, the last scene of all, there is nothing like this in *Antony and Cleopatra*. It makes its effects in quite a different way.

Shakespeare's technique of short scenes lends itself to a number of expressive purposes. In the first place, the practice of clearing the stage every hundred lines or so forbids – in the first movement of the play, at least – any very deep emotional engagement on the part of the audience. The constant changes of location (Egypt, Rome, Misenum, Syria, Athens), the contrasting evaluations of Antony's behaviour, as well as the **fluctuating** play of mood within the individual personality, all work to encourage an **ironical comparative response**, not quite detachment (because the play **kindles** a keen interest), but not a profound attachment of feeling either. The setting of the play is the entire world – the Roman empire and its **Levantine** neighbours, which *is* the world as its inhabitants see it. The dramatist may show us, in one scene, what is going on in that part of the world, but we can be sure that elsewhere, in many other places, many other things are also going on. From its opening scene the play establishes the simple fact that there are as many viewpoints as there are human beings. This is one of the points made by the scene, hardly necessary to the plot, in which Antony's lieutenant Ventidius is shown in Syria (III.I). We have scarcely met him before, and never see him again, but for a few moments we see Antony and Caesar through his eyes – and from this angle they look different. Public actions will always be interpreted in different ways, since every human being brings his own experience to what he sees, and what he sees may not be instantly intelligible to him. Indeed in this world, for all the **crystalline** clarity of the play's poetic

Glossary

circumscribed limited

fluctuating constantly changing

ironical comparative response a response that notices how one scene undermines or clashes with another

kindles arouses

Levantine Eastern Mediterranean

crystalline crystal-like; transparent

vision, human beings are intelligible neither to each other nor to themselves. Everyone moves in a mist of passion, driven by obscure pressures which may erupt in action seemingly involuntary. In the first scene Antony rejects the messengers, declaring himself wholly for Cleopatra and love. In the second, his mood has changed: he is all for breaking away and returning to Rome. When he takes leave of Cleopatra in the following scene he protests his **fidelity**, and in Act I, scene 5, we hear that he is still doing so through messengers. As soon as he arrives in Rome, however, he enters into a new understanding with Caesar and promptly agrees to marry his sister. We next see him assuring Octavia that he is a reformed man: 'that to come | Shall all be done by th'rule.' But a few moments later he has accepted his Egyptian destiny: 'I'th'East my pleasure lies' (II.3.6–7 and 41). Throughout the first half of the play the technique of short scenes is essential for putting across this view of human activity, with its stress on **discontinuity** and **multiplicity**, **volatility** and impulsiveness.

One effect of this technique, then, is to induce a moderately critical and ironical frame of mind: we keep on making comparisons. But there are other effects too. The short scenes are often **atomistically** constructed: they are often made up of even shorter discrete parts. In Act IV, scene 4, for example, Antony is shown going out to battle. The scene, though very short (under forty lines), contains several distinct units of action: Antony, in high spirits, is helped into his armour by Cleopatra; he is then greeted, first by a single soldier, and then by a number of '*Captains and soldiers*'; he takes a soldier's leave of Cleopatra and leads away his men; finally, alone with Charmian, Cleopatra muses on Antony's chances and shows that her real mood is one of low-spirited, clear-eyed detachment: 'Then Antony – but now. Well, on.' Such a technique makes possible a kind of quick close-up view of the speakers like the abruptly discontinuous shots of a news-reel. An illusion of intimacy is created, although we seldom if ever penetrate beneath the surface or overhear a speaker's unspoken thoughts. At the same time the illusion of life in free spontaneous motion is very powerful: the action becomes a succession of moments with a dream-like vividness. This is what life seems like, preserved in memory – brilliant snapshots surrounded by darkness.

From Emrys Jones, 'Introduction' *Antony and Cleopatra*, 1977.

fidelity   faithfulness; loyalty

discontinuity   lack of rational connection; breaks or interruptions

multiplicity   great number and variety

volatility   tendency to change suddenly

atomistically   made up of many small components

3 Time and timelessness in *Antony and Cleopatra*

Tanner discusses the different ideas of time that we get from Antony and Cleopatra. *In Egypt, time often seems suspended – or perhaps the leading characters wish it were so. In the wider world, ruled by Rome, historical events hurry onwards. He discusses how Roman ideas of time and an Egyptian state of timelessness clash in the play.*

There is a great stress on 'time' in *Antony and Cleopatra*, and it is well to remember that this is a history play. The outcome of the events it dramatized was the so-called 'Augustan peace', during which Christ was born and the **pagan** Empire – which **Virgil** called the Empire without end – was established, according to later writers, as a divine preparation for the Christian Empire. Octavius Caesar, himself a pagan, unknowingly laid the way for the True City, so in Christian terms the struggles and battles in the play affect, not merely his society, but all human society, the *orbis terrae* of Augustine. The events of the play are indeed of 'world' importance – world-shattering, world-remaking (the word 'world' occurs at least forty-five times in the play). By the same token, an earlier pagan world is being silenced, extinguished, and history – as the audience would know – is on Caesar's side. He is in time with Time. Antony and Cleopatra are out of time, in more than one sense. Thus, at the beginning, when Antony decides that he must return to Rome, Cleopatra silences his apologies, referring to the time-out-of-time when they were together – 'Eternity was in our lips and eyes' – while Antony, thinking Romanly for the moment, refers to 'the strong necessity of time'. Egypt, in this play, is a timeless present, which is to say an Eternity.

It can hardly escape our attention that the play is full of messengers from the start – two in the first scene, some thirty-five in all, with nearly every scene having a messenger of some kind. The play itself is extremely episodic, with some forty-two scenes (no scene breaks at all in the Folio), which makes for a very rapid sequence of change of place. There are nearly two hundred entrances and exits, all contributing to what **Dr Johnson** called the 'continual hurry' and 'quick succession' of

Glossary

pagan non-Christian

Virgil Ancient Roman poet (70–19BC)

orbis terrae Latin phrase referring to the world

Dr Johnson Samuel Johnson (1709–84) wrote a number of poems, essays and literary criticism but is perhaps best known for producing the first *Dictionary of the English Language* in 1755

events, which 'call the mind forward without **intermission**'. This can all be interpreted in different ways, but it certainly depicts a world in constant movement, in which time and place move and change so quickly that the whole world seems in a 'hurry' and in a state of **flux** – fluid, melting, re-forming. Messengers and messages bring information from the outside – they are interruptions, **irruptions, precipitants** of change. History is going on, and on, and at an ever accelerating pace. Yet the remarkable thing is that time seems somehow to stand still in Egypt – both within and without the reach of 'messages'; both vulnerable to history yet outside it. When Antony is away, Cleopatra simply wants to 'sleep out this great gap of time' (I, v, 6). (When she first approaches Antony in her 'barge', the city goes out to see her, leaving Antony alone 'Whistling to th' air; which, but for vacancy,/Had gone to gaze on Cleopatra too,/And made a gap in nature' – II, ii, 222–4. It is as if Cleopatra creates 'gaps' – gaps in time, gaps in nature.) For Rome, Egypt represents a great waste of time while the 'business' of history is going on. The word 'business', more often than not, carries **pejorative** connotations in Shakespeare. It is notable that Caesar interrupts his formulaic (as I hear it), **elegiac** 'praise' of the dead Antony because of – a messenger: 'The *business* of this man looks out of him;/ We'll hear him what he says' (V, i, 5o: my italics). He never completes the speech. Conversely, Cleopatra interrupts history to complete her poetic re-creation of Antony – from which no 'business' can distract her. From the Egyptian perspective, history itself is a 'gap of time', and Cleopatra, though growing physically older ('wrinkled deep in time'), seems to linger in Eternity, waiting for Antony to return from the trivial – though world-shattering – distractions of history.

From Tony Tanner, in *Prefaces to Shakespeare*, 1993.

intermission break	**precipitants** heralds; triggers
flux instability	**pejorative** unpleasant
irruptions sudden entrances	**elegiac** mournful

Section C: *Hamlet*
1 Memory and remembrance in *Hamlet*

> This extract highlights the prominence in Hamlet *of memory and acts of remembrance, of various kinds. These centre on the figure of Hamlet's dead father, whose ghost is a personification of the past, creating in Hamlet feelings of loss and of a duty to commemorate.*

Hamlet never promises to revenge, only to remember.

The language of this play is full of 'memory' and its **cognates**. Hardly has it begun than it pauses to celebrate Old Hamlet as a representative of that lost and epic age in which political issues were decided by fierce, single combat, an age unlike that in which kings take power by poison and combat is a courtly exercise played with **bated foils**. After the nunnery scene, Ophelia recalls a lover whom we have never really known ('O, what a noble mind is here o'erthrown!' (III. ii. 150–61)), while the ballads which she sings in madness, remembering Polonius ('His beard was as white as snow, | All flaxen was his pole, | He is gone, he is gone . . .' (IV. v. 195–7)), are equally loyal to the past. Such memories divert and slow the play, giving it an eddying, onward inclusiveness which contrasts with the movement of Shakespeare's other tragedies and which significantly departs from the remembrance-driven **dialectic** of *The Spanish Tragedy*. Set against these recollective impulses, others appear more selfish. Though he admits that 'The memory' of his brother is 'green', Claudius insists on 'remembrance of ourselves' (I. ii. 1–2, 7). Rosencrantz and Guildenstern accept from him 'such thanks | As fits a king's remembrance' (II. ii. 25–6). And Fortinbras winds up the tragedy by saying: 'I have some rights, of memory in this kingdom, | Which now to claim my vantage doth invite me' (V. ii. 389–90).

Such true, false, and cynical remembrances all reflect on the play's chief link with the past. Even before he sees the ghost, the prince remembers his father. When he first meets Horatio, for example, he almost sees the apparition which his friend has come to announce:

> *My father – methinks I see my father.*
> Horatio   *Where, my lord?*
> Hamlet   *In my mind's eye, Horatio.*
> Horatio   *I saw him once, 'a was a goodly king.*
> Hamlet   *'A was a man, take him for all in all,*
>   *I shall not look upon his like again.* (I. ii. 184–8)

Hamlet fends off his friend's recollection of the public man – the shared, 'goodly king'. His words advertise a privacy which remains his throughout the play. We can show that remembrance haunts him, even to the point of madness, and call this the heart of his mystery. But that heart can never, as he assures Guildenstern, be plucked out. In memory, Hamlet eludes us. Plainly, however, his words to Horatio are consistent with a degree of suffering. Even when comfort is found in the past, that only makes the present more desolate, 'an unweeded garden | That grows to seed' (I. ii. 135–6).

Glossary

cognates other words closely related to it
bated blunted
foils swords used for fencing
dialectic conflict

The Spanish Tragedy play by Thomas Kyd which is regarded as one of the first Revenge Tragedies

In bereavement, as the psychologist John Bowlby observes, 'because of the persistent and insatiable nature of the yearning for the lost figure, pain is inevitable'.* It is a measure of the prince's anguish that loss produces an exaggerated estimate of 'the lost figure'. Old Hamlet becomes 'So excellent a king, that was to this | Hyperion to a satyr;… Heaven and earth, | Must I remember?' (I. ii. 139–43). Claudius calls his nephew's dejection 'unmanly', accusing him of 'obstinate condolement' (93–4). But he is not two months bereaved of a noble father, buried and replaced in the queen's bed with scandalous dispatch. In any case, we know that Hamlet, healthily enough, is trying to shake off at least part of the burden of his father's memory.

For the 'tenders' of 'affection' made to Ophelia 'of late' – which can only mean since his return from Wittenberg for the funeral of his father† – show the prince attempting to replace a dead love-object with a living one. His inky cloak is ambiguous: a mark of respect for his father, it also indicates his desire eventually to detach himself from him. As **Freud** points out in 'Trauer und Melancholie', mourning has a psychical task to perform: to detach the survivor's memories and hopes from the dead. A combination of things prevents Hamlet from effecting that 'severance' which Helena (in a related play of 'remembrance') achieves even before the action of *All's Well that Ends Well* gets under way. Despite her Hamlet-like garb of mourning, her first soliloquy (reversing the prince's) admits that, because of her devotion to Bertram, 'I think not on my father . . . I have forgot him' (I. i. 79–82). Ophelia's apparent rejection is one factor in Hamlet's distress: by returning his letters and refusing him access she throws his love back onto the father who has never (it would seem) emotionally betrayed him. Another is Claudius' refusal to let him return to school in Wittenberg: this leaves the prince surrounded by people and places which remorselessly remind him of the dead king. But most important, of course, is the injunction, 'Remember me!' With this command the ghost condemns Hamlet to an endless, fruitless 'yearning for the lost figure'. In the nunnery and closet scenes, we see the effect on his sanity.

'My lord,' says Ophelia, 'I have remembrances of yours | That I have longed long to redeliver. | I pray you now receive them' (III. i. 92–4). This confirms for Hamlet a suspicion bred of his mother's 'o'er-hasty marriage', that woman's love is brief and unworthy. It seems that Ophelia wants to divest herself of every shred of attachment. In this she is no better than Gertrude, glad to forget her first husband. Moreover, the girl's gesture, 'There, my lord' (III. i. 101), recalls an earlier situation: Old Hamlet, like Ophelia, had pressed on the prince remembrances that were too much his already. In saying her farewells, Ophelia is, in effect, forcing him to remember (and no doubt, though an instrument of Polonius' plots, she *does* want to reclaim his attention). Through the loss of Ophelia, Hamlet feels that of his father – which is why the hysteria which follows is in excess of its apparent object. The sexuality which the prince **denounces** is that of his mother as well as Ophelia; Claudius, as well as he, is an 'arrant knave'; and there is indeed a sad resonance to the question – whether or not Polonius' surveillance is suspected – 'Where's your father?' (129). 'Hysterics', wrote Freud and **Breuer**, *'suffer mainly from reminiscences.'*

From John Kerrigan, in *Revenge Tragedy: Aeschylus to Armageddon*, 1996. (*First published in 1980*).

*John Bowlby, *Loss: Sadness and Depression* (Basic Books, 1980), p. 26

†I. iii. 91, 99–100

Freud Sigmund Freud (1856–1939), an Austrian neurologist and the founder of psychoanalysis

denounces condemns openly

Breuer Josef Breuer (1842–1925), an Austrian physician who developed the talking cure which led on to psychoanalysis

2 Hamlet: Avenging his father or saving his mother?

> *Adelman finds that Hamlet's principal concern is not revenge for his father, but complex feelings towards his mother. His fears about her sexuality and maternal power create a desire to purify her, to convert her from sin. For Adelman this accounts for the delays in the revenge plot and the centrality of the closet scene. Understanding Gertrude as a source of imaginings and anxieties more than an independent character also helps to account for the puzzles surrounding her character and her knowledge of her husband's murder.*

Hamlet initiates the period of Shakespeare's greatest tragedies because it in effect rewrites the story of Cain and Abel as the story of Adam and Eve, relocating masculine identity in the presence of the adulterating female. This rewriting accounts, I think, for Gertrude's odd position in the play, especially for its failure to specify the degree to which she is complicit in the murder. Less powerful as an independent character than as the site for fantasies larger than she is, she is **preeminently** mother as other, the intimate unknown figure around whom these fantasies swirl. She is kept ambiguously innocent as a character, but in the deep fantasy that structures the play's imagery, she plays out the role of the missing Eve: her body is the garden in which her husband dies, her sexuality the poisonous weeds that kill him, and poison the world – and the self – for her son…

Hamlet's father has become unavailable to him, not only through the fact of his death but through the complex **vulnerability** that his death demonstrates. This father cannot protect his son; and his disappearance in effect throws Hamlet into the domain of the engulfing mother, awakening all the fears **incident** to the primary mother–child bond. Here, as in Shakespeare's later plays, the loss of the father turns out in fact to mean the psychic domination of the mother: in the end, it is the specter of his mother, not his uncle–father, who paralyzes his will. The Queen, the Queen's to blame.

This shift of agency and of danger from male to female seems to me characteristic of the fantasy-structure of *Hamlet* and of Shakespeare's imagination in the plays that follow. The ghost's initial **injunction** sets as the prime business of the play the killing of Claudius; he specifically asks Hamlet to leave his mother alone, beset only by the thorns of conscience (1.5.85–87). But if Gertrude rather than Claudius is to blame, then Hamlet's fundamental task shifts; simple revenge is no longer the issue. Despite his **ostensible** agenda of revenge, the main psychological task that Hamlet seems to set himself is not to avenge his father's death but to remake his mother: to

Glossary

preeminently mainly or to a very great degree

vulnerability openness to emotional or physical hurt; lack of protection

incident relating

injunction command

ostensible apparent

remake her in the image of the Virgin Mother who could guarantee his father's purity, and his own, repairing the boundaries of his selfhood. Throughout the play, the **covert** drama of **reformation** vies for priority with the **overt** drama of revenge, in fact displacing it both from what we see of Hamlet's consciousness and from center stage of the play: when Hamlet accuses himself of lack of purpose (3.4.107–10), of failing to remember his father's business of revenge (4.4.40), he may in part be right. Even as an avenger, Hamlet seems motivated more by his mother than by his father: when he describes Claudius to Horatio as "he that hath kill'd my king and whor'd my mother" (5.2.64), the second phrase clearly carries more intimate emotional weight than the first. And he manages to achieve his revenge only when he can avenge his mother's death, not his father's: just where we might expect some version of "rest, perturbed spirit" to link his killing of Claudius with his father's initial injunction, we get "Is thy union here? / Follow my mother" (5.2.331–32).

This shift – from avenging the father to saving the mother – accounts in part for certain peculiarities about this play as a revenge play: why, for example, the murderer is given so little attention in the device ostensibly designed to catch his conscience, why the confrontation of Hamlet with Gertrude in the closet scene seems much more central, much more vivid, than any confrontation between Hamlet and Claudius. Once we look at "The Murder of Gonzago" for what it is, rather than for what Hamlet tells us it is, it becomes clear that the playlet is in fact designed to catch the conscience of the queen: its challenge is always to her loving posture, its accusation "A second time I kill my husband dead / When second husband kisses me in bed." The confrontation with Gertrude (3.4) follows so naturally from this attempt to catch her conscience that Hamlet's unexpected meeting with Claudius (3.3) feels to us like an interruption of a more fundamental purpose. Indeed, Shakespeare stages 3.3 very much as an interruption: Hamlet comes upon Claudius praying as he is on his way to his mother's closet, worrying about the extent to which he can **repudiate** the **Nero** in himself; and we come upon Claudius unexpectedly in the same way. That is: the moment that should be the **apex** of the revenge plot – the potential confrontation alone of the avenger and his prey – becomes for the audience and for the avenger himself a lapse, an interlude that must be gotten over before the real business can be attended to. It is no wonder that Hamlet cannot kill Claudius here: to do so would be to make of the interlude a permanent interruption of his more fundamental purpose. Not even Hamlet could reasonably expect to manage his mother's moral **reclamation** immediately after he has killed her husband.

From Janet Adelman, 'Man and Wife Is One Flesh: *Hamlet* and the Confrontation with the Maternal Body', 1992.

covert   secret; hidden

reformation   change for the better

overt   open; visible

repudiate   deny; reject

Nero   Roman Emperor 37–68AD, reputedly a cruel man and ruler who killed a number of people, including his own mother, to gain power

apex   peak; climax

reclamation   the act of reclaiming or getting something back

3 The complexity of Hamlet

The great nineteenth-century essayist Hazlitt argues that we are all of us Hamlets because in that character, Shakespeare created someone who has felt, and lived through, the whole range of human emotions. Hamlet the character embodies humanity in all its complexity, and thereby reflects the full breadth of Shakespeare's concerns. He examines his own thoughts and actions in a way that we cannot help but identify with.

It is the one of Shakespear[e]'s plays that we think of the oftenest, because it **abounds** most in striking reflections on human life, and because the distresses of Hamlet are transferred, by the turn of his mind, to the general account of humanity. Whatever happens to him we apply to ourselves, because he applies it so himself as a means of general reasoning. He is a great moraliser; and what makes him worth attending to is, that he moralises on his own feelings and experience. He is not a common-place pedant. If *Lear* is distinguished by the greatest depth of passion, HAMLET is the most remarkable for the ingenuity, originality, and unstudied development of character. Shakespear[e] had more **magnanimity** than any other poet, and he has **shewn** more of it in this play than in any other. There is no attempt to force an interest: every thing is left for time and circumstances to unfold. The attention is excited without effort, the incidents succeed each other as matters of course, the characters think and speak and act just as they might do, if left entirely to themselves. There is no set purpose, no straining at a point. The observations are suggested by the passing scene—the gusts of passion come and go like sounds of music borne on the wind. The whole play is an exact transcript of what might be supposed to have taken place at the court of Denmark, at the remote period of time fixed upon, before the modern refinements in morals and manners were heard of. It would have been interesting enough to have been admitted as a by-stander in such a scene, at such a time, to have heard and witnessed something of what was going on. But here we are more than spectators. We have not only 'the outward pageants and the signs of grief'; but 'we have that within which passes shew.' We read the thoughts of the heart, we catch the passions living as they rise. Other dramatic writers give us very fine versions and paraphrases of nature; but Shakespear[e], together with his own comments, gives us the original text, that we may judge for ourselves. This is a very great advantage.

Glossary

abounds is plentiful; has a lot of

magnanimity generosity

shewn shown

The character of Hamlet stands quite by itself. It is not a character marked by strength of will or even of passion, but by refinement of thought and sentiment. Hamlet is as little of the hero as a man can well be: but he is a young and princely novice, full of high enthusiasm and quick sensibility—the sport of circumstances, questioning with fortune and refining on his own feelings, and forced from the natural bias of his **disposition** by the strangeness of his situation. He seems incapable of deliberate action, and is only hurried into extremities on the spur of the occasion, when he has no time to reflect, as in the scene where he kills Polonius, and again, where he alters the letters which [Rosencrantz] and Guildenstern are taking with them to England, **purporting** his death. At other times, when he is most bound to act, he remains puzzled, undecided, and sceptical, **dallies** with his purposes, till the occasion is lost, and finds out some pretence to relapse into **indolence** and thoughtfulness again. For this reason he refuses to kill the King when he is at his prayers, and by a refinement in malice, which is in truth only an excuse for his own **want** of resolution, defers his revenge to a more fatal opportunity, when he shall be engaged in some act 'that has no relish of salvation in it.'

> 'He kneels and prays,
> And now I'll do't, and so he goes to heaven,
> And so am I reveng'd: that would be scann'd.
> He kill'd my father, and for that,
> I, his sole son, send him to heaven.
> Why this is reward, not revenge.
> Up sword and know thou a more horrid time,
>   When he is drunk, asleep, or in a rage.'

He is the prince of **philosophical speculators**; and because he cannot have his revenge perfect, according to the most refined idea his wish can form, he declines it altogether. So he **scruples** to trust the suggestions of the ghost, contrives the scene of the play to have surer proof of his uncle's guilt, and then rests satisfied with this confirmation of his suspicions, and the success of his experiment, instead of acting upon it. Yet he is **sensible** of his own weakness, taxes himself with it, and tries to reason himself out of it.

From William Hazlitt, 'Hamlet', 1916. (*First published as 'Hamlet' in 1817*).

disposition a person's usual temperament or frame of mind

purporting intending; with the design of bringing about

dallies deals lightly; delays

indolence laziness; idleness

want lack

philosophical reasonable, wise or learned

speculators thinkers; people who wonder about the outcome of their actions

scruples hesitates about what is morally right

sensible aware

Section D: *King Lear*

1 Language and female power in *King Lear*

> Rutter argues that the play explores deep anxieties about female power in relation to language, hence her comparison of women's tongues to the eels mentioned by the Fool in Act 2, Scene 4: they would not stay down in the paste to be eaten alive. Lear's daughters will similarly not be silenced. Meanwhile Lear himself is made to seem womanish by his tears and cursing. Rutter suggests that, at the time, these were associated with women, who wept or cursed because they had no real power.

Meanwhile, **patriarchal** anxieties about **effeminization** are played out with a vengeance in this most complicatedly feminized of all Shakespeare's tragedies. To begin with, Lear's story seems "overwhelmingly about fathers and their paternity" (in Janet Adelman's phrase) yet from first to last **adumbrates** "fantasies of maternal power." The theater, whose materializing practice is the **reification** of fantasy, embodies these fantasies: it gives its audience a long, hard look at them. What the audience sees in *Lear* is a series of disturbed images of the feminine that plays upon Lear's daughters even when they are off-stage, images that turn back upon men a terrible **inquisition**. At the beginning there is the recollection, relayed as a smutty joke whose punchline keeps being deferred, of "whoreson" Edmund's absent mother – a recollection from which Gloucester conveniently erases himself, only to have his role in the "sport" rematerialize in its retelling, as the stage picture makes male banter the site of (social) intercourse. At the end, there is a recollection, bizarrely recomposed, of the **Pietà**, Lear-as-Mary staggering onto the stage, arms full of Cordelia-as-Christ – a recollection whose **grotesquerie** challenges pity with the memory of paternity once disclaimed but now lavished upon the broken body of this **redemptive** child in whom the father at last professes himself to be well pleased. In between, the maternal is **reviled** (while the only hope the play offers to the future generation of man is that men should "grow pregnant to good pity"). The womb is "the dark and vicious place," the "sulphurous pit" that "is all the fiend's," all revulsion – "pah, pah" – all "burning, scalding, / Stench, consumption." Lust in the loins drives man to the fire where the mother incinerates him, dust to dust.

Glossary

patriarchal relating to a society in which men ruled over women

effeminization taking on the characteristics of a woman

adumbrates outlines; foreshadows

reification making something real or concrete

inquisition interrogation; aggressive questioning

Pietà work of art depicting the dead Christ being held by the Virgin Mary

grotesquerie distorted image

redemptive to be made a better person by being freed from sin

reviled condemned

Of course, the mother works by water, too. Lear knows his tears make a woman of him and that his daughters, causing him to weep, are to blame for having "power to shake my manhood thus."

He is both right and wrong. His tears of **impotent** rage are indeed the sign of the female. But Lear unmanned himself much earlier when, recoiling from Cordelia's refusal to mother his boyhood, he **appropriated** women's discourse: he fell to cursing. Cursing is the language of political exclusion. It is impotence, frustration **rhetoricized**. Yet it is threatening because it calls into being the ideas of a **Fury-ous** authority beyond the male control or political practice. Women curse. They curse because they cannot act. The scold, the **shrew**, the witch, the **drab**, all curse. Lear, cursing, is one of them. What he does not understand, however, is that his curses will be effective.

Lear's elder daughters neither weep nor curse. They do not need to. For, from the opening scene when they are authorized to "Speak" they begin the **reactive** process to Lear's effeminization. Having learned his language to survive his love test, they now assume the male voice, the male space Lear abandons. He dissolves into tears, they grow hard of heart. He rushes into the wilderness; they claim the castle seat. His words fail:

> *I will have such revenges on you both*
> *That all the world shall—I will do such things,*
> *What they are, yet I know not, but they shall be*
> *The terrors of the earth.*   (2.4.277–80)

"Pah, pah!", "Howl, howl, howl!" The daughters gain "large" speech. They manage words: "I will not speak with him"; "I'd have it come to question"; "I would breed from hence occasions, … / That I may speak." Managing words, they manage their father: "Deny to speak with me! Dost thou understand me, man?. … The King would speak … the dear father / … speak."

King Lear keeps coming back to the issue of speech and silence. So does my analysis, because what I want to say about the daughters returns constantly to their speech and to their speech withheld and to the opposition between speech and silence that the play always constructs as an opposition between mouth and heart. The eel pie of my title figures the daughters' tongues. It is a grotesque image, an ugly image. But then the play makes the daughters ugly: the two who speak are monsters; the one who does not is monstered. I begin, then, with an interrogation of narrative strategy – Lear's command that his daughters should speak – put against cultural practice, the audience's expectation that good women keep their mouths shut. These ideas are held in tension, but they are further challenged by their position in the theater, for the theater's **stock-in-trade** is speech; its practices and strategies are **inimical** to silence. What, then, does it mean in this theater to say "Nothing"?

From Carol Rutter, 'Eel Pie and Ugly Sisters in *King Lear*', 1997. (*First published as same in 1995*).

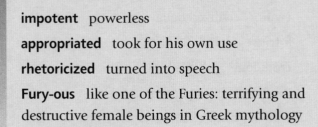

impotent powerless

appropriated took for his own use

rhetoricized turned into speech

Fury-ous like one of the Furies: terrifying and destructive female beings in Greek mythology

shrew bad-tempered woman

drab prostitute

reactive responding to another action

stock-in-trade something constantly used by a professional or an institution

inimical unfavourable; hostile

2 Ways of speaking in *King Lear*

In Kermode's view this play, so full of pain and injustice, wrestles with human suffering and evil on a universal, apocalyptic scale. Its uses of language form an integral part of the way it explores good and evil. The power of Cordelia's 'nothing', when she refuses to join her flattering sisters, needs to be seen in the context of a play in which language strains to find words to express the pain of being.

In *King Lear* we are no longer concerned with an ethical problem that, however agonising, can be reduced to an issue of law or **equity** and discussed **forensically**. For *King Lear* is about suffering represented as a condition of the world as we inherit it or make it for ourselves. Suffering is the consequence of a human tendency to evil, as inflicted on the good by the bad; it can reduce humanity to a **bestial** condition, under an apparently indifferent heaven. It falls, insistently and without apparent regard for the justice they so often ask for, so often say they believe in, on the innocent; but nobody escapes. At the end the punishment or relief of death is indiscriminate. The few survivors, **chastened** by this knowledge, face a desolate future. The play demands that we think of its events in relation to the last judgement, the promised end itself, calling the conclusion an image of that horror (V.iii.264–65).

Apocalypse is the image of human dealings in their extremity, an image of the state to which humanity can reduce itself. We are asked to imagine the **Last Days**, when, under the influence of some Antichrist, human beings will behave not as a rickety **civility** requires but naturally; that is, they will prey upon themselves like animals, having lost the protection of social restraint, now shown to be fragile. The holy cords, however "**intrinse**," can be loosened by rats. Gloucester may be **credulous** and **venal**, but his murmurings about the state of the world, which do not move Edmund, reflect the mood of the play: "in cities, mutinies; in countries, discord; in palaces, treason; and the bond crack'd 'twixt son and father … We have seen the best of our time" (I.ii.107–12). The voices of the good are distorted by pain, those of the bad by the coarse excess of their wickedness.

The rhetoric of the play is accordingly more explicit, less ambiguous, except – and it is admittedly a large exception – in the apparent unreason of the Fool and Poor Tom and the ravings of the mad King, where the imaginations of folly flood into the language and give it violent local colour. These **wild linguistic excursions** come later; the opening scene is in cool, even bantering prose, but as

Glossary

equity fairness

forensically in minute detail

bestial animal-like

chastened subdued; tamed

Apocalypse the end of the world

Last Days the Last Judgment in the Bible

civility civilized behaviour

intrinse tightly tied

credulous gullible

venal easily corrupted

wild linguistic excursions unconventional, colourful language

always in Shakespeare, it achieves much more than mere **exposition**. **Coleridge** understood its depth; the opening conversation between Gloucester and Kent makes it plain that Lear has already arranged the "division of the kingdom" before the ceremony in which he formally announces it, which was therefore intended to be less the declaration of a secret intention ("our darker purpose" [I.i.36]) than a self-gratifying charade. Lear can already be seen as **imperious** and selfish; we discover that even giving his kingdom away is a selfish act. And immediately we are offered a critical view of the other main sufferer, Gloucester, and his relations with his natural son, Edmund. Gloucester treats Edmund's birth as an occasion for bawdy joking and does not explain why, unlike his legitimate brother, Edgar, he should have been so long absent or why "away he shall again" (32–33). All this has much to do not only with their characters but with the nature of the ensuing action in so far as it depends on the folly of Gloucester and the ingenious **unregenerate** wickedness of Edmund.

Such economical writing is perhaps no more than should be expected of a dramatist in his prime. The ceremonial love competition that follows of course requires verse. The verse of the daughters Goneril and Regan has to be formal, **manifestly insincere**. Goneril is using what rhetoricians called "the topic of inexpressibility," standard fare in the eulogy of kings and emperors – "I love you more than words can wield the matter, / Dearer than eyesight … A love that makes breath poor, and speech unable …" (55–60). Regan follows with the well-established topical formula that **Ernst Curtius** calls "outdoing," or the *cedat-***formula**—"let her yield": her sister has expressed Regan's sentiments quite well, "Only she comes too short" (72). Cordelia, coming third in order of praising, would have a hard task, but shuns this competition, meaning nevertheless to outdo her sisters by exposing their **rhetorical falsity**. She would prefer to be silent, but the only way to announce that intention is to speak about it, which she does. She does not come out of the **archaic** and artificial contest well, defeated by the genuineness of her love, as France recognises; but she is far from passively yielding.

exposition laying out of the context; scene-setting

Coleridge Samuel Taylor Coleridge (1772–1834) was an English poet, critic and philosopher who, with Wordsworth, founded the Romantic Movement.

imperious arrogant; domineering

unregenerate unreformed; unrepentant

manifestly insincere obviously hypocritical

Ernst Curtius German literary scholar (1886–1956)

*cedat-***formula** a rhetorical device, meaning 'let her give way': Regan tries to outdo Goneril in her praise of their father

rhetorical falsity Cordelia refuses to play her sisters' game, aiming instead to expose the hypocrisy in their speechifying.

archaic old-fashioned; antiquated

Lear   ... *what can you say to draw*
        A third more opulent than your sisters'? Speak.
Cor   *Nothing, my lord.*
Lear   *Nothing?*
Cor   *Nothing.*
Lear   *Nothing will come of nothing, speak again.*   (85–90)

She does speak again, but virtually only to say nothing. Here **rhetorical formulae** are used for a dramatic purpose. The rage of the King confirms that he cannot be **temperate** in the absence of ceremony; the love he seeks is the sort that can be offered in formal and subservient expressions, and he therefore rejects the love of Cordelia and of Kent. The rest of the scene is equally well **contrived**. The style of personal pronouns is worth attention: Lear is almost always, regally, "we," until he loses his temper with his daughter, when he uses "I". Kent is truly "unmannerly," freely addressing the King as "thou": "What wouldest thou do, old man? ... Reserve thy state, / And in thy best consideration check / This hideous rashness" (146–51).

From Frank Kermode, *'King Lear'*, 2000.

rhetorical formulae established set of words used in speeches

temperate mild; controlled

contrived devised

3 The morality of *King Lear*

O'Toole describes how King Lear *upsets any comfortable moral assumptions on the part of the audience. In order to show this he focuses on the ending of the play, which seems to undermine the lessons that the play has set out to teach.*

Conventional complaints about the ending of the play – that there is no convincing re-assertion of the moral and social order at the end – forget that this is precisely the effect that Shakespeare structured the play in order to achieve. For the ending of the play is in a sense a second ending. We have already had a conventional, moral ending, the one provided by the single combat of Edmund and Edgar. In this fight, good beats evil, the conventional moral triumph is completed. It is an ending like the ending of any number of Shakespeare plays. Except that it is not the end, that it is not enough, that we are suddenly faced with this old man who comes back on stage, literally howling.

Edgar's killing of Edmund in 5, 3 has all the signs that it is the end of the play. Everybody is concerned to tell us that it's all over. Edmund confesses his sins and says 'Tis past, and so am I.' Edgar draws the handy moral of the story, the brothers are reconciled to each other. Edmund says 'The wheel is come full circle; I am here', which is as much to say 'the story is over now'. Albany comes in to pick up the pieces and to be the figure of some kind of order at the end. Edgar tells us about Gloucester's death: all the plot lines are being wrapped up. But then he says 'This would have seemed a period… but…' This should have been the end, but… It is the biggest *but* in theatrical history. Things start to go wrong with the moral ending in which good has vanquished evil. Edgar tells us about his encounter with Kent in terms which we cannot take to mean anything other than that Kent is dead. Eight lines later, Edgar tells us casually 'here comes Kent', Kent wanders in, and the conclusion refuses to conclude. The man we thought was dead is back on stage looking for Lear. We are brought back from the brink of a comfortable conclusion, forced to remember Lear and his suffering. Then, *'Enter Lear with Cordelia in his arms.'* Shakespeare, as Stephen Booth has put it, 'presents the culminating events of his story after his play is over'. The story bursts out beyond the moral ending of the play, the overwhelming sense of injustice breaks through the even balancing of good and evil. And this isn't a failure of the play: it is the whole point of the play's structure.

There is no simple sense of morality – of what is virtue and what is vice – in *King Lear*. Take a very simple virtue, one on which the whole **feudal society** from which Shakespeare's times are only beginning to emerge is founded: loyalty. The loyalty of the servant to the master, of the **serf** to the lord, is a basic moral category in those times. Does *King Lear* endorse that morality or deny it? It does neither: it shows morality falling apart under the stress of the play's traumatic events and emotions. In the figure of Kent, who is loyal to his king even though treated outrageously by him, the play may seem to contain a relatively simple idea of faithful service. But it is an ideal that is utterly insufficient to the ferocious demands of the play. Goneril's loyal servant Oswald, for instance, is a moral wretch. The servant who kills Cornwall, on the other hand, breaks a lifetime's trust – we are told that he has been in Cornwall's service since he was a child – but on any human scale he is clearly a vastly better person than Oswald. The traditional morality of loyalty, of knowing one's place and keeping it, is no longer of much use.

From Fintan O'Toole, '*King Lear*: Zero Hour', 2002. (*First published as same in 1970*).

Glossary

feudal society system in medieval Europe under which social relationships were based on land ownership in exchange for military service or labour

serf peasant labourer

Section E: *Othello*
1 *Othello*: The portrayal of Iago

This extract deals with the moral dilemma posed for audiences by Shakespeare's portrayal of Iago, who may be evil but is also witty and perhaps the cleverest person in the play. He resembles some of Shakespeare's comic characters even though his humour is wicked. The character of Iago therefore invites a complex and divided theatrical response that may conflict with our moral condemnation of him.

Liar, betrayer, mental torturer of Othello and Desdemona, murderer: if Iago were a straightforward villain he would arouse little **fellow feeling** in audiences, yet of course he is anything but straightforward and audiences have responded to him in different ways, depending on the actor. Readers, too, have disagreed. 'The character of Iago is so conducted, that he is from the first scene to the last hated and despised.' **Dr Johnson**'s verdict was echoed by Bradley, who reacted to 4.2.112ff. with 'burning hatred and burning tears' (197). Not so **Charles Lamb**: 'while we are reading any of [Shakespeare's] great criminal characters – Macbeth, Richard, even Iago, – we think not so much of the crimes which they commit, as of the ambition, the aspiring spirit, the intellectual activity which prompts them to overleap those moral fences.'

There is much to be said on both sides. In the theatre our reactions are unlikely to remain the same 'from the first scene to the last'; they fluctuate, and may come close to sympathizing with a villain. Dramatic perspective can even make us the villain's accomplices: he confides in us, so we watch his plot unfolding from his point of view. This happens in the novel as well: in *Crime and Punishment* we tremble with Raskolnikov, the murderer. A good actor grips the audience more completely, being in control of timing: he dictates the mode of impact of his wickedness and can whirl the audience off its feet, whereas a reader controls his own timing.

Iago enjoys another important advantage, that he is the play's chief humorist. Most of Shakespeare's major characters are endowed with their own brand of humour (Falstaff, Touchstone, Hamlet, Lear; Rosalind, Viola, Cleopatra); Iago's, though related to the humour of **Aaron** and Richard III, is also quite distinctive. W. H. Auden called him 'the joker in the pack', a

Glossary

fellow feeling sympathy; agreement

Dr Johnson Samuel Johnson (1709–84) was a poet, essayist, moralist and critic who compiled *A Dictionary of the English Language* (1755), which had a far-reaching effect on modern English.

Charles Lamb English writer and essayist (1775–1834) best known for the children's book *Tales from Shakespeare*

Crime and Punishment 19th-century Russian novel by Fyodor Dostoyevsky

Aaron 'Aaron the Moor' is the secret lover of Tamora and responsible for the downfall of the Andronicus family in *Titus Andronicus*.

'practical joker of a peculiarly appalling kind', partly because Emilia speaks of him as her 'wayward husband' and 'she must know Iago better than anybody else does'. Yet *wayward* does not mean joker (see 3.3.296n.), and Auden's loose label really identifies one of Iago's convenient masks, not the inner man, and may blind readers to Iago's essential sadism. His humour either intends to give pain or allows him to bask in his sense of his own superiority; very rarely is it at his own expense (contrast Falstaff, Cleopatra, etc.), and it is never merely delightful, as is Rosalind's or Puck's. When Iago says 'Well: happiness to their sheets!' (2.3.26) he deliberately **defiles** Cassio's image of Desdemona; deciding whimsically that it scarcely matters who kills whom –

> *Now, whether he kill Cassio*
> *Or Cassio him, or each do kill the other,*
> *Every way makes my gain*
>
> (5.1.12–14)

– he enjoys a godlike sense of power. In 2.1.100–60 we see Iago at his most playful; the impression that he *simply* enjoys himself, having fun and being sociable, is overshadowed by our awareness that he 'crowds' his companions, and then suddenly cancelled when he reveals, in soliloquy, that he hates the social games he took part in.

Nevertheless, since his victims lack humour, Iago appeals to us as more amusing: dramatic perspective compels us to see with his eyes, and to share his 'jokes'. His humour also makes him seem cleverer than his victims. His cleverness, however, should not be exaggerated, as by Harold Goddard, an otherwise perceptive critic, who thought that Shakespeare bestowed 'the highest intellectual gifts' on Iago. This might be Iago's opinion, but hardly Shakespeare's. Iago excels in short-term tactics, not in long-term strategy. The possibility that his own despised wife may accuse him publicly of 'a lie, an odious, damned lie' (5.2.176) and send him to his death has not occurred to him. This is because, despite his cleverness, he has neither felt nor understood the spiritual impulses that bind ordinary human beings together, loyalty, friendship, respect, compassion – in a word, love. Emilia's love (of Desdemona) is Iago's undoing.

From E. A. J. Honigmann, 'Introduction' *Othello*, 2001. *(First published as same in 1991).*

defiles   corrupts; pollutes

2 The character of Othello

Leavis's highly influential interpretation of Othello refuses to believe in Othello's essential dignity and instead draws attention to his habit of self-dramatisation. He has not learned from his suffering and he does not really examine himself. On the contrary, argues Leavis, he dies still acting a part and relishing his own performance.

When he discovers his mistake, his reaction is an intolerably intensified form of the common 'I could kick myself':

> *Whip me, ye devils*
> *From the possession of this heavenly sight!*
> *Blow me about in winds! roast me in sulphur!*
> *Wash me in steep-down gulfs of liquid fire!*
> *O Desdemona! Desdemona! dead!*
> *Oh! Oh! Oh!*

But he remains the same Othello; he has discovered his mistake, but there is no tragic self-discovery. The speech closing with the lines just quoted is that beginning

> *Behold, I have a weapon,*

one of the finest examples in the play of the self-dramatizing trick. The noble Othello is now seen as tragically pathetic, and he sees himself as pathetic too:

> *Man but a rush against Othello's breast,*
> *And he retires. Where shall Othello go?*

He is ruined, but he is the same Othello in whose essential make-up the tragedy lay: the tragedy doesn't involve the idea of the hero's learning through suffering. The fact that Othello tends to sentimentalize should be the reverse of a reason for our sentimentalizing too.

For even, or rather especially, in that magnificent last speech of his Othello does tend to sentimentalize, though to say that and no more would convey a false impression, for the speech conveys something like the full complexity of Othello's simple nature, and in the total effect the simplicity is tragic and grand. The quiet beginning gives us the man of action with his habit of effortless authority:

> *Soft you; a word or two before you go.*
> *I have done the State some service, and they know't.*
> *No more of that. I pray you in your letters,*
> *When you shall these unlucky deeds relate,*
> *Speak of me as I am; nothing extenuate,*
> *Nor set down aught in malice . . .*

Glossary

stoic-captain leader who is dispassionate or philosophical

sufficiency an adequate amount

epigrammatic quotable; wise-sounding

Othello really is, we cannot doubt, the **stoic-captain** whose few words know their full **sufficiency**: up to this point we cannot say he dramatizes himself, he simply *is*. But then, in a marvellous way (if we consider Shakespeare's art), the emotion works itself up until in less than half-a-dozen lines the stoic of few words is eloquently weeping. With

> *then must you speak*
> *Of one that loved not wisely but too well,*

the **epigrammatic** terseness of the **dispatch**, the **dictated** dispatch, begins to quiver. Then, with a rising emotional swell, description becomes unmistakably self-dramatization – self-dramatization as un-self-comprehending as before:

> *Of one not easily jealous, but being wrought,*
> *Perplex'd in the extreme; of one whose hand,*
> *Like the base Indian, threw a pearl away*
> *Richer than all his tribe; of one whose subdued eyes,*
> *Albeit unused to the melting mood,*
> *Drop tears as fast as the Arabian trees*
> *Their medicinal gum.*

Contemplating the spectacle of himself, Othello is overcome with the pathos of it. But this is not the part to die in: drawing himself proudly up, he speaks his last words as the stern fighting man who has done the state some service:

> *Set you down this;*
> *And say besides, that in Aleppo once,*
> *Where a malignant and a turban'd Turk*
> *Beat a Venetian and traduced the state,*
> *I took by the throat the circumcised dog*
> *And smote him, thus.*   [stabs himself]

It is a superb *coup de théâtre*.

As, with that double force, a *coup de théâtre*, it is a peculiarly right ending to the tragedy of Othello. The theme of the tragedy is concentrated in it – concentrated in the final speech and action as it could not have been had Othello 'learnt through suffering.' That he should die acting his ideal part is all in the part: the part is manifested here in its rightness and solidity, and the actor as inseparably the man of action. The final blow is as real as the blow it re-enacts, and the **histrionic intent** symbolically affirms the reality: Othello dies belonging to the world of action in which his true part lay.

From F. R. Leavis, 'Diabolic Intellect and the Noble Hero', 1937.

---

dispatch   letter or report

dictated   said aloud to be written down

coup de théâtre   French term meaning sudden dramatic turn of events

histrionic intent   deliberately over-dramatic

3 *Othello*, race and society

The book from which this extract is taken was an important contribution to discussions of race and colonialism in relation to Shakespeare's plays. In the first part of this extract Loomba discusses how Othello *at once reinforces and questions early modern stereotypes of black people and Muslims. In the second part she explores the reputation of Venice as an open and cosmopolitan society, and how this might have been regarded in England as both a model and a warning.*

Othello is both a fantasy of interracial love and social tolerance, and a nightmare of racial hatred and male violence. In this play, a white woman flouts the established social hierarchies of 'clime, complexion and degree' to marry a black man, an act that betrays, in the eyes of some beholders, 'Foul disproportions, thoughts unnatural!' (3.3.235–8). Location, skin colour, and class are seen to add up to 'nature' itself. But the real tragedy of the play lies in the fact that these hierarchies are not external to the pair. Iago's **machinations** are effective because Othello is **predisposed** to believing his pronouncements about the **inherent duplicity** of women, and the necessary fragility of an 'unnatural' relationship between a young, white, well-born woman and an older black soldier. Ideologies, the play tells us, only work because they are not entirely external to us. Othello is a victim of racial beliefs precisely because he becomes an agent of misogynist ones.

The portrayal of Othello, the 'Moor of Venice' stands at the complicated **crux** of contemporary beliefs about black people and Muslims. As we have seen, black-skinned people were usually typed as godless, **bestial**, and hideous, fit only to be saved (and in early modern Europe, enslaved) by Christians. On the other hand, commentators such as Henry Blount wondered whether Muslims, with their tightly organized religion and sophisticated empires, were 'absolutely barbarous' or whether they had 'another kind of civility, different from ours'. Both blacks and Muslims were regarded as given to unnatural sexual and domestic practices, as highly emotional and even irrational, and prone to anger and jealousy; above all, both existed outside the Christian fold. *Othello* yokes together and reshapes available images of 'blackamoors' and Moors, giving us a black Moor who has both a slave past and a noble lineage, a black skin and thick lips as well as great military skill and rhetorical abilities, a capacity for tenderness as well as a **propensity** to violence…

The English saw Venice not simply as a place for female deviance, but also as an ideal republic and hub of international trade. Whereas female 'openness' was dangerous and immoral, political

Glossary

machinations plots or schemes

predisposed inclined or given

inherent duplicity natural deceptiveness

crux vital stage or point

bestial brutal or savage

propensity natural tendency

and **mercantile** openness was much admired by an England in search of overseas markets and colonies. Despite its Catholicism, Venice became an ideal that was **invoked** by English writers subtly to critique domestic affairs. In 1599, Lewis Lewknor translated into English Contarini's *Commonwealth and Government of Venice*, a work with which Shakespeare was familiar. This book helped **propagate** a 'myth of Venice' in England which exalted the city-state as an open but ordered society, a model of civility which informs Brabanzio's angry assertion: 'This is Venice | My house is not a grange' (1.1.107–8). Brabanzio's choice of words is ironic, for Iago tells him that in fact his house *has* become a grange in which a 'black ram', a 'Barbary horse' is 'tupping' his daughter (1.1.88, 89, 113). Venetian civility has been built by letting in the very foreigners who now threaten to undermine it at a different level. Because Othello is needed in order to combat the Turks, the Senate is willing to regard him as 'more fair than black' but for Desdemona's father such colour-blindness is not possible. Here we see a tension between the state and the family, although the two were so often equated in contemporary political **rhetoric**.

How might an English audience have reacted to the Senate's pronouncements? As discussed earlier, England was increasingly hostile to foreigners, both officially and at a popular level, and London had witnessed several major riots against foreign residents and **artisans**. Would this play have unsettled or reinforced such hostility?

Did the play make the case for a tolerant society, or did it issue a warning not only to disobedient daughters but also to 'open societies' who let in outsiders, especially black ones? It might be useful to recall that if some English writers extolled the virtues of Venice, others found Italy a dangerous model for the English: 'the religion, the learning, the policy, the experience, the manner of Italy' were the 'enchantments of **Circe**, brought out of Italy, to mar men's manners in England'. Thus Venice's openness could also be viewed as dangerous by a society itself fairly suspicious of outsiders.

From Ania Loomba, *'Othello* and the Radical Question', 1998.

mercantile   commercial; relating to trade or traders

invoked   called upon, usually for inspiration

propagate   spread or promote

rhetoric   speeches or oratory

artisans   craftsmen

Circe   Greek goddess of magic

We are grateful to the following for permission to reproduce copyright material:

Text

Extract on pages 6-7 from *A Companion to Shakespeare's Works: Vol. I: The Tragedies*, by David Scott Kastan, Blackwell, 2003, pp.7-9, copyright © 2003, CCC Republication; Extract on pages 8-9 from *Why Does Tragedy Give Pleasure?* by A. D. Nuttall, Oxford University Press, 1996, pp.1-2. Reproduced by permission of Oxford University Press; Extract on pages 12-13 from *Everybody's Shakespeare: Reflections Chiefly on the Tragedies* by Maynard Mack, University of Nebraska Press, 1993, pp,260-262, copyright © 1993 by Maynard Mack. Reproduced by permission of the University of Nebraska Press; Extract on pages 14-15 from *Shakespeare's Magnanimity, His Tragic Heroes Their Friends and Families* by Wilbur Sanders and Howard Jacobson, Chatto & Windus, 1987, pp.125-127, copyright © Wilbur Sanders and Howard Jacobson, 1978. Reproduced by permission of The Random House Group Ltd and Curtis Brown Group Ltd, London on behalf of Wilbur Sanders and Howard Jacobson; Extract on pages 16-17 from *Introduction Antony and Cleopatra* by Emrys Jones, Penguin, 1977, pp.26-28. Reproduced by kind permission of Dr Barbara Everett; Extract on pages 18-19 from *Shakespeare: The Greek and Roman Plays, Introduction from Tragedies: Volume 2 by William Shakespeare* by Tony Tanner, Harvard University Press, 1993, pp.631-632, copyright © the Literary Estate of Tony Tanner. Reproduced by permission of Professor Stephen Heath, Estate for Tony Tanner and Everyman's Library, an imprint of the Knopf Doubleday Publishing Group, a division of Random House LLC. All rights reserved; Extract on pages 20-21 from *Revenge Tragedy: Aeschylus to Armageddon* by John Kerrigan, Oxford University Press, 1996, pp.182-184. Reproduced by permission of Oxford University Press; Extract on page 21 from *Loss: Sadness and Depression* by John Bowlby, Basic Books, 1980, p.26. Reproduced by permission of Perseus Books Group; Extract on pages 22-23 from *Suffocating Mothers: Fantasies of Maternal Origin in Shakespeare's Plays* by Janet Adelman, Routledge/Taylor & Francis, 1992, pp.30-32, copyright © 1991, CCC Republication; Extract on pages 26-27 from 'Eel Pie and Ugly Sisters in King Lear' in *Lear: from Study to Stage: Essays in Criticism* by Carol Rutter, Fairleigh Dickinson University Press, ed James Ogden, 1997, pp.172-175. Reproduced by permission of Associated University Presses; Extract on pages 28-30 from *Shakespeare's Language* by Frank Kermode, Allan Lane, 2000, Penguin Books, 2001, pp.181-186, copyright © Frank Kermode 2001. Reproduced by permission of Penguin Books Ltd and Peters Fraser & Dunlop (www.petersfraserdunloip.com) on behalf of the Estate of Frank Kermode; Extract on pages 31-32 from *Shakespeare is Hard, But So Is Life: A Radical Guide to Shakespearean Tragedy* by Fintan O'Toole, Granta Books, 2002. Reproduced by permission of A P Watt at United Agents on behalf of Fintan O'Toole; Extract on pages 33-34 from *Othello* by E.A.J. Honigmann, Arden Third Series (Introduction) pp.38-40, Bloomsbury Arden Shakespeare, an imprint of Bloomsbury Publishing Plc, copyright © E.A.J. Honigmann, 2001. Reproduced with permission; Extract on pages 35-36 from 'Diabolic Intent and the Noble Hero' by F. R. Leavis, in *Scrutiny Magazine*, December 1937, pp.274-276. Reproduced with kind permission of Dr L. R. Leavis; and Extract on pages 37-38 from *Shakespeare, Race, and Colonialism* by Ania Loomba, Oxford University Press, 1998, pp.91-92. Reproduced by permission of Oxford University Press.